MY LITTLE EARTHMAN

VED NAIR

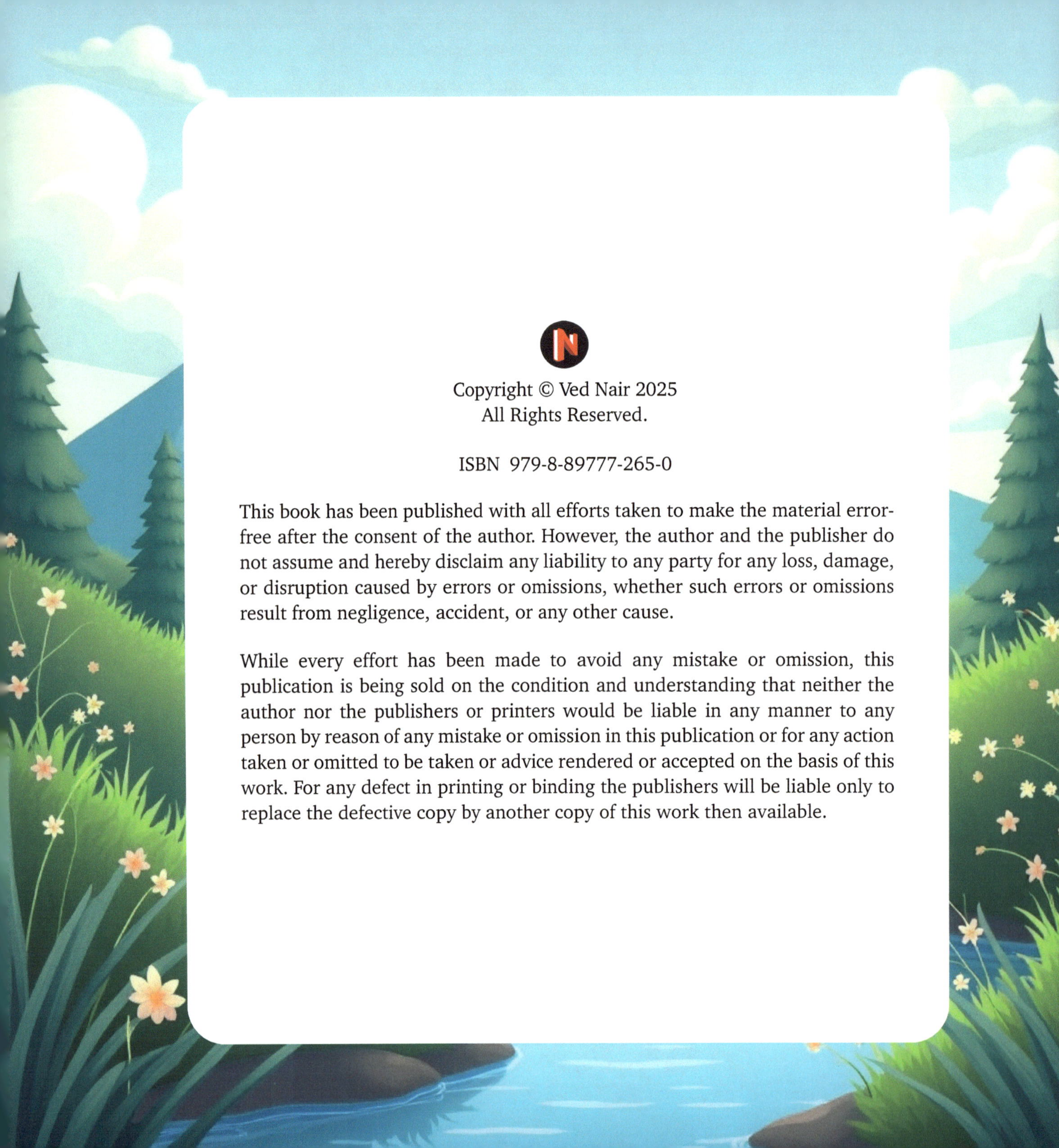

ISBN 979-8-89777-265-0

This book belongs to

How to Protect the Earth

Hello, my
Super Earthman: Did you know you can protect our beautiful planet? Yes, you! Let us learn how to be a Little Earth Hero!

Let Us Save our Water!

Let Us Save Our Water!
Can we turn off the tap while brushing our teeth? Drip, drop—no **water** wasted!

Love the Trees!

Love the Trees! Trees provide us with clean air to breathe, yet we cut them down to make tissue paper. Earthman, can we switch to hand towels instead and help save our trees?

Reuse, Recycle.
Pick Up, Clean Up!

Pick Up, Clean Up!
Earthman, did you see the trash?
Please help us put the waste in the right bin.

Lights Out!

Lights Out! Finished playing?
Let us turn off the lights before we leave the room… Shall we?

Plant a Friend!

Plant a Friend!
A tiny seed grows into a big tree. Trees are magical as they give us more RAIN. More Rain means more Water for everyone.

Reuse and Share!

Reuse and Share!
Old toys and clothes can find new homes. Sharing is caring for the Earth! So let us do that, my little Earthman!

Ride, Walk, or Roll!

Ride, Walk, or Roll! Cars make smoke,
but cycling and walking keep the air clean!
So, no more coughs for us!

No to Plastic!

No to Plastic! Skip single-use plastic straws, plates, spoons, and bottles. Instead, let's enjoy eating with our hands and carry our own water bottles when going out. By reusing what we have, we can keep our Earth happy and healthy!

THANK YOU FOR PROTECTING ME!

Hooray for You!
You are a Little Earth Hero now-**EARTHMAN!**
High five for helping our planet!

EARTHMAN CERTIFICATE

This Certificate is presented to:

for protecting our planet Earth as
"EarthMan"